UNDERSTANDING
HOW LAWS ARE MADE

BY MATT BOWERS

SEQUENCE

AMICUS | AMICUS INK

Sequence is published by Amicus and Amicus Ink
P.O. Box 1329, Mankato, MN 56002
www.amicuspublishing.us

Library of Congress Cataloging-in-Publication Data
Names: Bowers, Matt, author.
Title: Understanding how laws are made : American government / by Matt Bowers.
Description: Mankato, Minn. : Amicus, 2020. | Series: Sequence | Includes
  bibliographical references and index. | Audience: K to Grade 3.
Identifiers: LCCN 2018025938 (print) | LCCN 2018026766 (ebook) | ISBN
  9781681517544 (pdf) | ISBN 9781681516721 (library binding : alk. paper) |
  ISBN 9781681524580 (pbk. : alk. paper)
Subjects: LCSH: Legislation--United States--Juvenile literature. | Bill
  drafting--United States--Juvenile literature.
Classification: LCC KF4945 (ebook) | LCC KF4945 .B69 2020 (print) | DDC
  328.73--dc23
LC record available at https://lccn.loc.gov/2018025938

Editor: Alissa Thielges
Designer: Veronica Scott
Photo Researcher: Holly Young

Photo Credits: Shutterstock/MoDOG cover; Shutterstock/Sergey Kamshylin cover;
Shutterstock/VOJTa Herout 5; Getty/Bettmann 6–7; iStock/Steve Debenport 8; Getty/
Bloomberg 11; Getty/Hero Images 12–13; WikiCommons 14; www.congress.gov 15;
AP/J. Scott Applewhite 16–17; Getty/Congressional Quarterly 18; Getty/Jeff Greenberg
20–21; Getty/Tom Williams 22; Newscom/Hill Street Studios/Betty Mallorca Blend
Images 24–25; iStock/Rocky89 26; iStock/EvgeniyShkolenko 29

Printed in the United States of America

HC 10 9 8 7 6 5 4 3 2 1
PB 10 9 8 7 6 5 4 3 2 1

TABLE OF CONTENTS

Laws Rule! 4

Share an Idea 9

Congress Gets to Work 14

Over to the President 27

It's a Law! 28

Glossary 30

Read More 31

Websites 31

Index 32

Laws Rule!

What would you like to change about the world? For example, maybe it's cleaning up pollution. Or maybe you want to protect wild animals.

One way to change the world is to make a new law. Laws are rules made by governments. Cities and states have laws. There are national laws, too. Those are called **federal laws**. So how are federal laws created?

Laws can keep animals like red foxes safe.

LOADING . . . LOADING . . . LOADING . . .

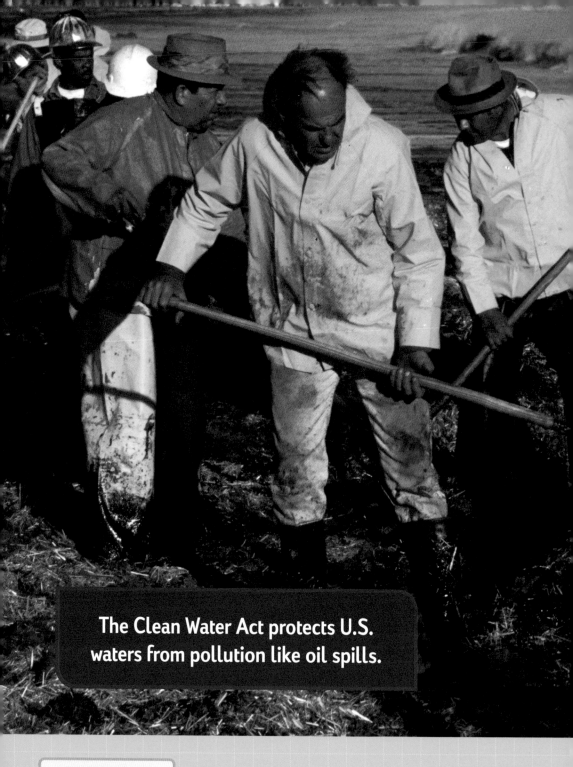

The Clean Water Act protects U.S. waters from pollution like oil spills.

Citizens think of an idea for a new law.

MONTH 1

LOADING . . . LOADING . . .

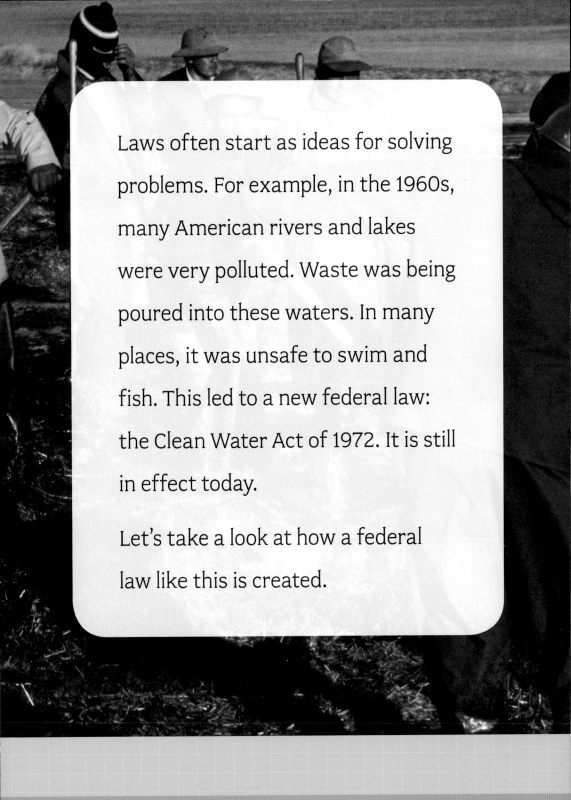

Laws often start as ideas for solving problems. For example, in the 1960s, many American rivers and lakes were very polluted. Waste was being poured into these waters. In many places, it was unsafe to swim and fish. This led to a new federal law: the Clean Water Act of 1972. It is still in effect today.

Let's take a look at how a federal law like this is created.

LOADING... LOADING... LOADING...

A citizen has an idea for a law.
She shares it with lawmakers.

Citizens think of an idea
for a new law.

MONTH 1 ⟶

ING . . . LOADING . . .

Citizens contact their
U.S. senators and U.S.
representatives.

Share an Idea

An idea is just the start. In order for it to become a law, people need to work with lawmakers.

The **U.S. Congress** makes federal laws. It has two chambers, the **Senate** and the **House of Representatives**. Senate members are called senators. House members are called representatives. Citizens contact lawmakers. They explain their idea for a new law.

A representative hears from citizens. She likes their idea for a new law. She agrees to help turn their idea into a **bill**. A bill is an idea for a new law written down. As the bill's **sponsor**, she will introduce it in the House. But first she has to write it.

> Bills can start in the Senate, too. A senator like Elizabeth Warren (right) can sponsor a bill.

Citizens think of an idea for a new law.

A representative writes a bill.

MONTH 1 ⟶ MONTH 3

. . . LOADIN

Citizens contact their U.S. senators and U.S. representatives.

Citizens think of an idea for a new law.

A representative writes a bill.

MONTH 1 → MONTH 3   MONTH 4

ADING . . .

Citizens contact their U.S. senators and U.S. representatives.

The bill gains support from other citizens.

Other people hear about the bill. They like the idea. They write letters to their representatives and senators, asking them to support it. Citizens organize meetings and marches. A **movement** starts. More citizens find out about the bill. They demand it becomes a law.

A woman signs a petition to show support for a bill.

G...LOADING...LOADING...

Congress Gets to Work

A bill can start in the House or the Senate. In the House, it is dropped in a box called the **hopper**. It is assigned a number. This tells Congress when the bill was received. The number helps track the bill's progress. Next, the bill goes to a committee for review.

HOPPER

Citizens think of an idea for a new law.

A representative writes a bill.

The bill is introduced in the House and sent to a committee.

MONTH 1 ⟶ MONTH 3   MONTH 4   MONTH 5

Citizens contact their U.S. senators and U.S. representatives.

The bill gains support from other citizens.

1 **SEC. 2. SECRETARY DEFINED.**

2   In this Act, the term "Secretary" m

AUTHENTICATED
U.S. GOVERNMENT
INFORMATION
GPO

Sec. 2. Secretary defined.

Sec. 101 °.

TITLE I—GENER^ PROVISIONS

resources development bills.
Fund to support navigation.
arbors.
n.

constructed dams.
s.
rs.

115TH CONGRESS
2D SESSION

H. R. 8

To provide for improvements to the rivers and harbors of the United States, to provide for the conservation and development of water and related resources, and for other purposes.

I

cretary.

Army Corps of Engineers.

cts by non-Federal inter-

projects by non-Federal

nt studies and projects.

IN THE HOUSE OF REPRESENTATIVES

MAY 18, 2018

Mr. SHUSTER (for himself, Mr. DEFAZIO, Mr. GRAVES of Louisiana, and Mrs. NAPOLITANO) introduced the following bill; which was referred to the Committee on Transportation and Infrastructure

ts.

AND RELATED

A BILL

To provide for improvements to the rivers and harbors of the United States, to provide for the conservation and development of water and related resources, and for other purposes.

1   *Be it enacted by the Senate and House of Representa-*

2 *tives of the United States of America in Congress assembled,*

orida.

RE

3 **SECTION 1. SHORT TITLE; TABLE OF CONTENTS.**

4   (a) SHORT TITLE.—This Act may be cited as the

5 "Water Resources Development Act of 2018".

6   (b) TABLE OF CONTENTS.—The table of contents for

7 this Act is as follows:

Sec. 1. Short title; table of contents.

Bills that start in the House begin with H.R. Senate bills begin with an S.

LOADING...LOADING...LOADING...

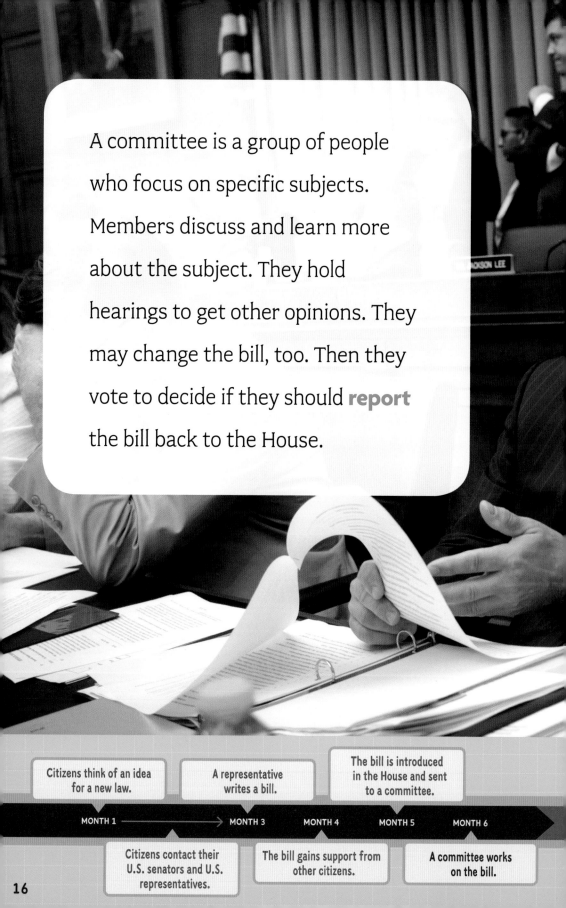

A committee is a group of people who focus on specific subjects. Members discuss and learn more about the subject. They hold hearings to get other opinions. They may change the bill, too. Then they vote to decide if they should **report** the bill back to the House.

Citizens think of an idea for a new law.

A representative writes a bill.

The bill is introduced in the House and sent to a committee.

MONTH 1   MONTH 3   MONTH 4   MONTH 5   MONTH 6

Citizens contact their U.S. senators and U.S. representatives.

The bill gains support from other citizens.

A committee works on the bill.

JOHNSON (GA)

A House committee does research. They discuss and share what they learn.

Citizens think of an idea for a new law.

A representative writes a bill.

The bill is introduced in the House and sent to a committee.

MONTH 1 ———→ MONTH 3   MONTH 4   MONTH 5   MONTH 6

Citizens contact their U.S. senators and U.S. representatives.

The bill gains support from other citizens.

A committee works on the bill.

The committee approves the bill! They send it to the House Chamber. This is a big room where the representatives meet. Now the House discusses the bill. Some people are for it. Others are against it. More changes are made. They want to use very specific language. That way, there is no confusion.

Representatives take their seats in the House Chamber.

Representatives debate the bill.

LOADING...LOADING...

Now it is time for the big vote. Representatives can vote by voice, by standing up, or by pressing a button. If more representatives vote for it than against it, the bill passes. This is called a majority vote.

The House passes the bill! It is now sent to the Senate.

Buttons record a representative's vote. "Yea" means yes and "nay" means no.

Citizens think of an idea for a new law.

A representative writes a bill.

The bill is introduced in the House and sent to a committee.

MONTH 1 — MONTH 3   MONTH 4   MONTH 5   MONTH 6

Citizens contact their U.S. senators and U.S. representatives.

The bill gains support from other citizens.

A committee works on the bill.

Representatives
debate the bill.

MONTH 8 ⟶

The House
passes the bill.

Citizens think of an idea for a new law.

A representative writes a bill.

The bill is introduced in the House and sent to a committee.

MONTH 1 ——→ MONTH 3   MONTH 4   MONTH 5   MONTH 6

Citizens contact their U.S. senators and U.S. representatives.

The bill gains support from other citizens.

A committee works on the bill.

In the Senate, the bill is sent to another committee. This committee changes the bill. It is now different from the one the House passed. The bill is then sent back to the Senate. The changes are debated. The senators vote. A majority of senators vote for the bill. It passes!

Senators carefully review proposed changes to a bill.

Representatives debate the bill.

The Senate changes the bill and passes it.

MONTH 8 ⟶ MONTH 10

. . . L O A D I N G . . .

The House passes the bill.

Citizens think of an idea for a new law.

A representative writes a bill.

The bill is introduced in the House and sent to a committee.

MONTH 1 → MONTH 3   MONTH 4   MONTH 5   MONTH 6

Citizens contact their U.S. senators and U.S. representatives.

The bill gains support from other citizens.

A committee works on the bill.

But wait! Now, the Senate bill and the House bill don't match. In the end, both chambers of Congress must pass the exact same bill. Members from each chamber work together. This group is called a conference committee. Good news! After a few days, they come to an agreement. The bill is now the same. It is passed in both the House and Senate.

Senators and representatives come together to create one bill.

Representatives debate the bill.

The Senate changes the bill and passes it.

MONTH 8 ⟶ MONTH 10   MONTH 11   ▸ADING...

The House passes the bill.

Conference committee works on bill; House and Senate pass same bill.

The president likes the bill. He signs it!

Citizens think of an idea for a new law.

A representative writes a bill.

The bill is introduced in the House and sent to a committee.

MONTH 1 ⟶ MONTH 3 MONTH 4 MONTH 5 MONTH 6

Citizens contact their U.S. senators and U.S. representatives.

The bill gains support from other citizens.

A committee works on the bill.

Over to the President

Now it's the president's turn. Many things can happen at this point. The president can sign the bill, making it a law. The president can also **veto** the bill. Congress can override a regular veto. This takes a two-thirds vote in both the House and Senate. Luckily, the president signs the bill.

Representatives debate the bill.

The Senate changes the bill and passes it.

The president signs the bill.

MONTH 8 → MONTH 10 MONTH 11 → N G . . .

The House passes the bill.

Conference committee works on bill; House and Senate pass same bill.

It's a Law!

The citizens' idea has passed. It's now a federal law! It will be enforced starting next year.

Creating laws can be a long process. Bills can go through many different paths before they are passed into law. For example, a senator can introduce a bill, too. But this is one way you can change the world for the better!

Citizens think of an idea for a new law.

A representative writes a bill.

The bill is introduced in the House and sent to a committee.

MONTH 1 ⟶ MONTH 3   MONTH 4   MONTH 5   MONTH 6

Citizens contact their U.S. senators and U.S. representatives.

The bill gains support from other citizens.

A committee works on the bill.

New laws can help the environment by reducing pollution.

| Representatives debate the bill. | The Senate changes the bill and passes it. | The president signs the bill. |

MONTH 8 → MONTH 10 MONTH 11 →

| The House passes the bill. | Conference committee works on bill; House and Senate pass same bill. | The citizens' idea is now a federal law. |

Glossary

bill An idea for a new law written down.

federal law A law made by the U.S. Congress for the United States.

hopper A box that bills are put in for consideration by the House.

House of Representatives One of two houses in the U.S. Congress composed of 435 voting representatives who make laws for the United States. The bigger a state's population, the more representatives it has.

movement A group of people who work to bring about change.

report When a committee sends a bill back to Congress.

Senate One of two houses in the U.S. Congress composed of 100 senators who make laws for the United States. Each state has two U.S. senators.

sponsor A representative or senator who introduces a bill.

U.S. Congress The U.S. government's legislative branch, which makes laws for the United States.

veto When the U.S. President chooses not to approve a bill.

Read More

Cane, Ella. *The U.S. House of Representatives.* North Mankato, Minn.: Capstone Press, 2014.

Connors, Kathleen M. *How Does a Bill Become a Law?* New York: Gareth Stevens Publishing, 2018.

Spalding, Maddie. *How the Legislative Branch Works.* North Mankato, Minn.: Child's World, Inc., 2016.

Websites

Learning Adventures – What is a Law?
https://bensguide.gpo.gov/a-what-is-law

Kids in the House – How Does a Bill Become a Law?
https://kids-clerk.house.gov/young-learners/lesson.html?intID=31

iCivics – LawCraft
https://www.icivics.org/games/lawcraft

Index

Clean Water Act 7
committees 14, 16, 19, 23
conference committees 25
Congress 9, 14, 25, 27

federal laws 4, 7, 9, 28

House Chamber 19
House of Representatives
9, 10, 14, 16, 19, 23, 25, 27

presidents 27

representatives 9, 10, 13, 19, 20

Senate 9, 14, 20, 23, 25, 27
senators 9, 13, 28
sponsoring 10

veto 27
veto override 27
voting 16, 20, 23, 27

About the Author

Matt Bowers is a writer and illustrator who lives in Minnesota. When he's not writing or drawing, he enjoys skiing, sailing, and going on adventures with his family. He hopes readers will continue to learn about government and be leaders in their communities.